I0083279

Shearsman

issues

63 & 64

Summer 2005

Edited by
Tony Frazer

Shearsman magazine is published by
Shearsman Books Ltd
58 Velwell Road
Exeter EX4 4LD
www. shearsman.com

ISBN 0-907562-48-5
ISSN 0260-8049

Acknowledgements:
We are grateful for the permission extended by various copyright-
holders to include some of the work published here: Alberto Blanco for
poems from his volume *El libro de las piedras* (Conaculta, Mexico City,
2003); Franz Hammerbacher and Edition Korrespondenzen, Vienna, for a
poem from *münden – entzüngeln* by Anja Utler, copyright © 2004, Edition
Korrespondenzen, Franz Hammerbacher; Suhrkamp Verlag, Frankfurt-am-
Main, for permission to print a poem by Peter Huchel from *Gezählte Tage*,
copyright © 1972, Suhrkamp Verlag; two poems by Lutz Seiler, one from *pech
& blende*, copyright © 2000, Suhrkamp Verlag, and one from *vierzig kilometer
nacht*, copyright © 2003, Suhrkamp Verlag; and four poems by Robert
Walser from *Das Gesamtwerk*, Vol. XI, edited by Jochen Greven, copyright
© 1985, Suhrkamp Verlag; Pio Serrano and Editorial Verbum, Madrid, for
the poems by Gastón Baquero from *Poesía Completa*, copyright © 1988,
Editorial Verbum. These poems were first published in *Magias e invenciones*
(Ediciones Cultura Hispanica, Madrid, 1984). The publishers
gratefully acknowledge the financial assistance of Arts Council
England with their 2005-2007 publishing programme.

Subscriptions and single copies:
Back issues, from issue 1 to 62, may be had for £3 each direct from the press.
From this double-issue onwards, each edition costs £7.50/$12.50 through
trade channels. Single copies can be ordered for £7.50 direct from the press.
A subscription, which now covers two of these new-size editions (where
the minimum page-count will be 80) costs £12 in the UK, £14 for the rest of
Europe, and £15 for the rest of the world. Longer subscriptions may be had
for a proportionately higher payment—this will insulate purchasers from
further price-rises during the term of the subscription. We cannot accept
payment in currencies other than pounds sterling, unless the purchaser adds
£7 or its equivalent to cover our bank charges. For large purchases (£75 or
more) however, this requirement is waived — in such cases, please contact
us for a quote on a package of titles, or a long-term subscription.

CONTENTS

Editorial   4

Frances Presley   5
Lisa Samuels   13
Robert Saxton   16
Gad Hollander   19
Philip Jenkins   25
Sam Sampson   32
Rupert M. Loydell   35
Gordon Kennedy   40
Sarah Law   45
Giles Goodland   48
Spencer Selby   53
John Seed   55

Gastón Baquero   58
    (translated by Mark Weiss)
Alberto Blanco   63
    (translated by Joan Lindgren)
Robert Walser   67
    (translated by Christopher Middleton)
Peter Huchel   71
    (translated by Harry Guest)
Lutz Seiler   72
    (translated by Tony Frazer)
Anja Utler   75
    (translated by Tony Frazer)

Biographical Notes   78

Recent & Forthcoming Publications   82

EDITORIAL

Some explanation is necessary for the radical change in the shape and size of this magazine. Until now it has been produced as cheaply as possible, in a small quarterly format intended to keep postage costs down. We were forced into a radical rethink by the fact that the cost of producing the 32-page version of the magazine four times a year had risen rapidly over the past twelve months. This had eroded the cost difference vis-à-vis a journal shaped like this and produced by the same method used for Shearsman Books titles – print on demand. Oddly enough, it is also cheaper to post this book-sized journal twice every year than it is to post the pamphlet-sized edition four times, notwithstanding the fact that this version carries more pages than two of the old-style magazines (84 v. 64). Subscription rates would have risen sharply in any event for the old-style magazine, and this new version now retails for approximately double the cost that would have had to be applied to single copies of the old one. The next issue will appear in October or November 2005 and will also run to 80-90 pages; it too will carry a double issue number, while we unravel existing subscriptions – all of which will be honoured.

For the past three years, each issue of the magazine has also been made available online; in future, about half of each new issue will go online—approximately one month after publication—and the selection will be representative, where permissions allow. *Shearsman* will continue to be open to submissions, but the extra page-count available in the new editions will be used to showcase some of our authors: thus in this issue, we are featuring Lisa Samuels and John Seed, who have new volumes published by Shearsman Books in April and May 2005.

FRANCES PRESLEY

March

On North Hill
for Tilla Brading

above Greenaleigh

lower buds
thinking without

Tilla, the tides
the tides
are always too early
or too late
to swallow
words
nowhere to lay them
on the beach

crests cannot
catch up
too many, white, commas
clustering
not spacing

on the path
white trainers of morning
her morning
of terracotta terrace
trend

ended heather
pressure
deeper blue
grounds
sea cloud
say it's dolphins

                                         back pack
                                            voices
                                        remind me
                                        of reading
                                       Martin Eden
                                      on this knoll
                                   disintegrating
                              edition and waiting
                                   for stragglers

or another burden

this great burden
on my back
will sink me
will sink me lower

these arms around my shoulders
these legs around my waist
between us
we carried
the twins

                    this great burden... from John Bunyan's *Pilgrim's Progress*

June

on North Hill

blind drawing

for Kelvin Corcoran

axial
fear bone
tender acorns
tender engines
probe frames
angular
tri angular
spot sun
is this blind drawing
and where?

warm fingers to lip
tidal surge and resurge
Colette sounds
thunder collect

broken bark
smoothes my face

a branch is forking down the clouds
turning pen into shadowline
and pylon
branches chased to sea

West, is where you're tending
he said

how do we survive the westward
surf culture
the fear of immigration
the fear of immigrant self?

not detachment
but embrace
and the interchangeability
of frames

real drawing is like this
and now I have made
the bridge too wide
the peak again
piercing the pubic bone
the public bone
rising

                                        Kelvin said
                            Just the sea, Frances

sur sur sur sur
sur surring

su   su   su   rus

October
on North Hill

bless test
mess of leaves
wings will not make

              serious
              back pack
              stride

fern returns
leaf crisps
clenched
hear
here

      ~   ~

break   stop   wave
make it   return
a flick of the wrist
she hasn't got
yet

      who has not built
      a house
      will now no longer
      will not build

                          no nay never
                          or some version
                          on the march
                          against
                          war

      no more
      builds now
      who has not yet
      who has not built
      yet builds now
      bilds

(this is the dialogue of memory)

bird rattle
sun slats
through dry leaves

like the turning
segments
of glass
at Foreland Point
occulting the optic

                                  white outriders
over ride the line

February   in St Michael's

the sound of the hoover:

                                (burrs
                       catches on skin
                 furs throat lining
                      sounds like
                 the line under
      the dead straight way)

turn around sound
catches its breath
bones and tiptones
the lining of my throat
the dust still vocal

        above
her hoover   movement
she is hovering
the altar
sun on green carpet

2

he was holding the kettle
above the birdbath
melting the ice

gold tipped wings
and straight back
against the low tree
holding their
(apple)
onyx

such an one and
such an one

beware the bullfinch
flat caps go flatter

3

pull
                              strike
pull

light lines across
the spiral steps

                    no
           admittance

no   trespass

                         step

                                   across

sun slats
through dry leaves

like the turning
segments
of glass
at Foreland Point
occulting the optic

                              white outriders

                                        over ride
                              the line

LISA SAMUELS

Something for you

Traditionally   harpers
build   fences
like   that   they   know
how   to   "disinvest"   –
or   taking   the   moment
further   than   measurement
we   could   call   it
soporific   sunshine   –
equivalent   your   eyes
getting   dimmer
by   the   year   folding
into   dromedary
lashes   –
under   conditions   we
know   how   to   distinguish
let's   say   the   present
has   no   presence
anyway   what   we   proffer
is   that   voice   rising
to   a   green   invective
still   within   the   leaf
like   piano-eyes
we   took   a   limb   tale
and   drew   it   backward
so   that   you   could   see
the   sketches   saying   "really
I   exist"   and   then
judge,   of   course,
for   yourself

Latitude

the circles rise up toward the air
they are transparent anyway
we look at them through human
hair, barbiturate of rapture

the air is fine of silk
through eyes, apparently
transfigured, refining through
the circular novitiate

the first day once again
assumes a beach, a sand
wealth temperance, I look at you
through human eyes
no different

(Longitude)

(your little feet
disrobe the light
with touches)

(or age itself is differential
lovely, as torpor
interrupts the night

of heat and feet
and lilting eyes
alike)

The end of distance

I've hardly taken to any life at all
that is a penchant for falling, a syllable
wreathed reckless on the air
that I don't mean, or measuring

has habited us to complicated beds
where we do or do not say the things
we are. I've taken to adjusting from afar

the work we vitalize or will not keep
among us like appropriated tasks
we spill our life across, wanting to watch

what happens when the will is washed
like blue jeans, tightens up, and holds us
clasply in its fit, our haunches rectified
uneven, like something proved by what we have not given.

ROBERT SAXTON

Voyaging

Seas are where you recognize
the pirates, or the flock or school
whose harsh yet neighbourly cries
lash a comfortable ridicule,

fins ploughing clay, turning the worm,
gulls nimble as English men o'war,
a buoy bolt-upright in the storm,
which then turns out to be more

like a weathercock, then indeed
a weathercock, on a drowned spire
undaunted by a white horse stampede,
or loss of the uplifting choir

damned by raiding pagan gospels.
Only oceans have cathedrals.

***

Woods are what vandals left behind
when they carried off the history prize.
They float like pondweed on the mind.
Their leaves are the republic's lies,

and grandma's hairnet, smiling gold,
all weathers' topsail, crow's-nest of straw.
She keeps the girls from growing old,
which keeps the boys from wanting more.

Virtue is cheeky, villainy po-faced,
luxury a mask, poverty a root.
The dry log's lettering in a rustic taste
charts sea-lanes blossoming with loot.

Forests are the limbo of the hatless drowned,
failed baptism, the stonefish wound.

The Flute Player

after Rumi

The flute
dismays
three birds

all sad
to hear
such cries

for its
dear nest
so far

away,
its bed
of reeds,

since they
had hoped
to hear

instead
how breath
can make

you see
a man
whose heart

throbs like
a bird,
showing

such skill
breath hops
with joy,

song-flight
of all
he loves

and not
nine holes
of pain,

deep wish
to fly
back home,

though both
clipped wings
and all

free breath
just tell
you this:

he's lost,
hollow,
empty,

farther
from the
source than

ever –
whence all
music.

GAD HOLLANDER

from 'Theatre of Psychodialysis'

Black Love
to misr-em-ember

> ... *but don't be surprised, my feuding friend,*
> *my enemy, seized by black love,*
> *if the groans of love will be the groans of torture,*
> *kisses – tinged with blood.*

Nikolay Gumilyov, tr. Richard McKane

if that is what we call love
that persistent yearning to touch
like a river's to change course
the star of redemption

physique de l'amour
a lamp leaning forward like her face /
in a forgotten town
out of prison or the army
gazing at the sun a forlorn young man
seedy part of town
american is talked here
your heartstrings hear its familiar strains

a soft oblivion around your weathered skin
its text open to the air
'for we are but of yesterday
and know nothing because our days upon earth are a shadow'

underexposed the heart hidden forever
a shower of solace on a carpet of citrus blossom
three times the hands obscure the face
three times the hands reveal the face

first impressions last but have no right to stop
no right to mine nostalgia
a veil of joy over his face a delicate grin
a state of sporadic animality
every word I say devoured by a voracious ghost inside you
I'm a burning juniper
endless longing
time is running out

caress her in that tender vein
the flight you undertook
biblical behest
her naked body

the chinese poet shunned by men
had to play his jade flute to the gods' silent congress
there are beings some human some divine
from whom we need to maintain our distance

it's raining outside
the awareness of a stone or a blade of grass
as if reality were quite simply excess weight
a sandbank of incomprehension
the confounding syllable wedged like a thorn between creation and
exhaustion
the vessel through which the longing is expressed
the intensity of a word correctly chosen and precisely placed
an angel without a visa among the damned.

***

New York, 1958: black love, dark courtyard, noises faraway, beyond the
sooty fire-escapes.

Berlin, 1938: black love, dark courtyard, footsteps at my heels. God
flees.

London, 1978: black love, dark courtyard, she prostrates herself at the
plinth of a statue. The next year there is famine, and the year after that,

too. God makes a connection between infinity and death, filling the synapse.

Lisbon, 2008: black love, dark courtyard, hysterical voices at the windows swallowed by a voracious earth. She is wearing black, o un-angel, and her feet are quiet, dusty and bare.

Paris, 2038: black love, dark courtyard, glancing at her sodden shoes in the rain, she reminisces about what had been, what might have been, what had never been. The old grow nostalgic for the very old, and God is falling through the wet air.

London, 2001: black love, dark courtyard, a glass of red wine opposite another, talk of hard times once, and intimations of times to come, her mouth in black & white like an old TV. The evening chill at his back.

Sinai, 2004: black love, dark courtyard, an improvised street corner, he holds up a sign that reads "I am God." It means: Help Wanted. Nobody applies. It is the year of the nouvelle cuisine famine. Ice-cream melts down the gutters in the middle of the streets. A woman walks past and says: "You have the capacity to be happy." Parched, dry as the space between the sentiment she speaks and the cliché that marks it. The signs multiply. Black love, dark courtyard, o un-angel, a man was broken in obscurity.

★★★

I suffer but I enjoy the pain. Suffering is my ambrosia; I savour it with a sense of purpose – to overcome pain. Once my masochistic thirst has been quenched, I descend from above and wander among mortals. But when I see your pathetic grovelling, your feeble genuflection at the foot of my statue, I grow homesick for pain and long to suffer again. No sooner do I arrive than I'm compelled to leave, to escape through clouds and return to my suffering. I suffer in dark, away from it all. That's how I like it. At the heart of my pain is my yearning for your stupid humanity. I don't always express such yearning quietly, there are times when I wail in the night. You've heard me, black love, you've hurt me. A full moon opens my larynx. Black love, I love women and men, I love animals of every species, and I love the stars and every speck of dust in the universe. I cry under a full moon, my throat open, my fingers urgently stroking your vulva, teasing the tears out drop by drop, offering my pain for your pleasure. Yes I love women, so much, my voice fading in garbled intimacy. I love supermodels as I love supernovae, each class rousing a unique desire. But I suffer for love, too. Women I love for their form and their cool solar warmth, and supernovae for the climax of their blinding intelligence; yet when I hold one in my arms the other shyly retreats into a vacuum, and the absence of either tortures me as if I were being flayed. I love women because their soul is anchored in a sea of love where I drown perpetually, my breath expelled forever in its depth, and I love the stars in the sky because each foretells the secret place of my drowning; I hear it at night when I lean my head on its womb. In my dark I see you, black love. I've tasted seed between your thighs and roamed inside your eyes for light. I've stroked your eyebrows with my fingers and my lips have kissed the downy brow of your sex. I've smiled on your nose that tilts this way or that and have closed my mouth on your breast like an infant. I've held your hand like a god, my desire was divine, my soul mythic, my love full of disquiet. I want to replenish your breasts with milk, to fill your womb with honeycomb, to provide you with the agonies of childbirth, so that when you cry I will cry and when you laugh I will laugh. In my dark, black love, I see you, and you are beautiful in my eyes.

SLOW FADE IN FROM WHITE:

EXT. DAY. THE SUN IN A CLOUDLESS SKY. OVEREXPOSED.

If I say you... you know, you are, you is ambiguous. So what should I call you, black love, lurking in the foreground of thought, shy in the depths of oblivion, adrift among the false shadows of dreams? I want to distinguish the no from the no, extinguish the yes in the embers of light. I want, and you want, and we are lost.

And light – that filter we place over dark to defer a certain cast of nostalgia... I don't remember light in its proper genetic shape. It is said to have a magical, frivolous quality and to excel at capturing the moment, any moment, before releasing it to view. Do you agree, black love? And do you remember? Are you nodding behind your starched apron in that celestial kitchen? My thoughts encircle your absence, a disembodied presence, beyond whose extremes I can taste flesh as I approach reality, peering over its take-away counter – a breast, a thigh, the vapid skin of chicken parts dipped in sizzling oil – and then retreat, lower my eyes, submerge them in your smell, close them on your thigh, your breast, your sable skin, engage them in the aura of your difference, collect them in a dream.

***

I told you about Benjamin of Tudela, the Spanish Jew who travelled East, weaving his way around the Crusades. And about Jacob of Ancona, who travelled to China before Marco Polo. I mentioned the latter through a breath of love, the words on my tongue plying your labia, my mouth enfolded in flesh, an exotic scent compounding my meaning as the wet delirium of expectancy climbed the ladder to heaven. I could tell by that sweet swelling smell you believed every word; and I at least wasn't lying, only repeating what I had heard, prone with my ear to your thigh, my memory tenderly creeping into your heart, your heart dilating like the pupils of your eyes in a surging desire to swallow light as light died away, while my tongue distended into your deepest torments.

***

Torture is poetic, a discourse of ambiguity rising through a wellspring of pain. Victim or perpetrator, we identify with it completely, accept its frisson, settle into its anticipation. Unlike murder, torture has no cause or effect; on either side of pain, titillation, anxiety, humiliation, depth of gratitude, clarity's cruelty and other psychological titbits circle like slow planets. Torture is a misty hope lifting out of hopelessness; we call it beautiful or ugly, misnaming it in a brutal revenge. You love to torture me; I in turn love to be tortured by you. This is all we know, our love of pain and pleasure. Our respective ideologies are at odds with each other, but we step back from the brink, we do not desire each other's annihilation; only submission is at stake, a gift of the last giving. We might abolish the pain or enhance the pleasure, or opt for a dreamless sleep, but given or taken, our pain is more pleasurable than nothingness. This is our fear. Torture is the most savoury form of love;

we could build a religion out of it were we not blinded by the acuity of pain, deafened by the purity of heard or unheard screams. We are implicated in torture as in our own civilisation; if we deferred on it we would recognise ourselves as inhuman. This is our shame, from which we hide in the garden.

Merchants of light, peering into the dark and bringing good tidings with them, tarnish our solitude and join our mouths together in a profitable parody of – what's the word after ineffable?

***

We talked and we talked, talked till dawn or till dusk, talked till midnight or noon, and watched the moon and the sun and the stars ignoring our talk. We watched the trees and the couples under the trees exchanging essential rumours of love. We talked until language got tired, atrophied and turned back on itself, enfolded in silence, lulled by an easy seduction. And silence spread herself wide like a whore, sucking each syllable out of our talk and becoming big with meaning. But what were we trying to say?

Now we're homesick and don't know which way to turn. But we talk and we pray. We pay silence her fee and then talk some more. And as night arrives on the scene we fall asleep in the deepest sleep and dream out our love, and our talk issues out of the dark, incomprehensibly, passing over us in an alphabet of shooting stars from an unknown language.

w

PHILIP JENKINS

cairo   book 3

1.

ground bass

a thin light
beneath the door
taut, expectant

the starched edge of a
conversation carried on
into the afternoon.

2.

lustral water spilled
on the paving stone
unsettled desire

the chord probes
a network of aching recognitions

structures the movement

3.

how is it here   dark have
here and wet   wave after
wave wash insipidly over

unwarmed tea slops fleshless and forward
a wake and backwash   thinly a
soup, emeto-cathartic, erasing
everything a stain

now, here a trace egested
dark and wet have here an impress
a gradual becoming

4.

from dark light to dark light
acircle of shadows

an exhalation of dank evening
grips the gloved root

ashes on the sand
the throat at night

5.

the finger held up
equivocates its understanding
farther from myself at least nine
miles on from it
the hours of unusual disparity

the banquet table deserted
explores the frozen limitations
the borderland of its own unease

6.

my face precarious now, the mirror propinquent
holding my breath, I buoy up
rising through mud, opening to the air, my skin
stretches out, freed from primordial chaos

my lips part, rip open as twin companies
dividing in military exercise
breathe out the word (inside)
the world (outside) congeals

7.

visual image:
     down on the floorboards, a telephone
     rings continuously

audial image:
     footsteps on the floorboards move
     from right to left and repeat

each image partakes of the undifferentiated
a slice of bread pulled through the egg yolk

8.

the note resonating slightly
puckers into infinity

vegetation recovers the landing stage
an inheritance of tin work
copper rivets   fortune trespasses
on its military past

distance dilates the reflection
variegates perspective

9.

the back of the hand examined
in front of the face the
space between
dematerialises

a formulation preserved entire
precipitance lacquered into place
the hem shrivels

the cracks connecting subject
to object   small implosions
snap brittly   the indistinct grin
at the centre of dumb motion

(London, 1982)

Four Poems

going up country

the trembling woodsman
appears in double exposure

with borrowed moustache
and faded dungarees

waiting by the hayloft
all the latest kinds of hay

every variety of hay
and some deformed vegetables

the tractor left out in the field to rust
and we to explain the process

our sorry attempts to do so
are childlike but reassuring

the greenhouse overlaps the tractor slightly
at this point in our explanation

when it comes into focus again
it will be time to move on from the country

where gnats baffle in warm air
my forearm dancing through

riding through texas

I am used to them, their
difficult natures, stopping
only once en route just
to ask the way to amarillo

and searching through drawers
of all this underwear I
thought I'd forgotten about

and here they all are again

now like each new line
written out making life
uncomfortable
for those gone before

I am crossing the brazos at waco
I am wearing my coonskin cap
in memory of the alamo and of

my tennessean great grandmother
who made it for me although it
didn't have a tail

but too late, too late, all you
things I shall be

remembering
today for the last time

a last guinness with vito

The greatest friend I had in life
is hidden from me now
— Mike Heron

the canvas silent, the leaves
retained details of past

conversations we shared
a torch shone over them

words no less difficult to read
I planted rosemary in memory

chewed quietly on a twig
together we had felt

at home and at once
the sunlight tasted

different like the garden
carries on talking

and it does too,
butterflies rippling

along the cut surface

neither the quay

  slowly the bus overtakes
  eventually the boat
that delivers bananas I
  think it is

behind white double doors
something we cant see

just happened at least that's
how we recollect

ambulance sirens, swallows
wheeling overhead, the white ball

careering across the snooker table
effortlessly, the invention of stereo

next doors yard, a small bonfire
sputtering to a close, these

and all other things taking place
here together, myself included

SAM SAMPSON

Streamlined Mechanics

Celerity describes an ideal interface

symmetrical, dolphins arc: a surface breaks,
traceable, swallows dip: motion points.

Hollow lines often bend towards the central thought
the cerebral artifice where waves alternate

energetic, the impish flow starts at a high-angle pulse
(the spill produces significant secondary drag)

glide : swivel : push-off

our thrust-generating limbs are inherently unsteady: to accent, butterfly the stroke,
back, or breast; we are mechanistic, transient in this steady-state submergence.

Cetaceous, blood fills the air-water interface: breathless, we blow...locomotion.

Millefiori

i.m. Michael Donaghy

Pastiche, we plant paperweight scenes,
a flower fits its cyclic tricolour (blue, white, red...

a thousand blooms)

white, forget-me-nots; words which manufacture blue

not stellar red, sacred, or lily white
but felt light: the bruise of tempered craze.

Orpheus at Whatipu

The entrance signals where wavelengths break

at the outskirts of motion, the entrance sings
rising, falling, rising...sounding into sequence.

Sometimes it blinds the horizon to be looking back.

Red on black

two variable oystercatchers circle this shipwrecked scene,
the sun detonated; constellations torching the surface wake.

RUPERT M. LOYDELL

Sunflower

'Everything is a guide,
I had thought
But then the world would be here
Only to keep us from becoming lost'
– 'The New Season', James McCorkle

apocalyptic end of things   final line conclusion
scrambling how time works   learning how to fly
constant failure to levitate   pushed into slow descent
lurking in the shadows   tiny closet of a room
real chemistry at work   radical translation
reincarnation of some sort   poems of my own making

backwards through art history   sequences or series
silent conversations   more coherent speech
find out information   make up your own mind
overhaul the alphabet   progress forward now
artificial intelligence   an awful thing to say
discover where we are going   luring people away

carpeted from wall to wall   edited start to finish
outrageous and high-handed   gonna walk all over you
forming its own structure   moving through the room
hostile to performance   make the world my own
brief instances of darkness   comets in the sky
laws of love and pity   rockets to the moon

diversity and access   contents of the mind
misplaced sense of importance   emotionally attached
exclamation-marked horizon   attempting to belong
field trips and rock formations   articulate aloud
exploring unlit passages   ambition's constant charm
weathered skylights black with age   spray painting in the dark

everything is mentioned   but there is no real proof
forgotten footnotes in the text   diverse community
slight differences of detail   revolution's end
would have to be repeated   could not be otherwise
always illness or accident   inflicting harm by glance
no taboo on looking   be silent do not touch

familiar as wooden piers   splinters in every tree
expert in dramatic productions   sad and backward glance
elderflower tea and strawberry wine   chestnuts and walnuts too
dynamite theologians   looking after spiritual needs
after argument or visit   things begin to improve
walk about the streets alone   centre of the world

grand corridors of power and glass   past is common to us all
you get to play the hero then   write the final scene
conjure up demons and wizards   beauty of water's song
four minutes to cross the river   secret travel plans
chained to the gates of the palace   buried alive in a tomb
no mourning or apology   death is terminal

hopscotch involves a pattern of squares   sent messages reach mum
nobody must break the chain   keep quiet about the corpse
oak trees are safe in electric storms   belong to both and neither world
the plumbing is in disarray   we nearly got washed away
love comes from being vulnerable   a memory of popular songs
rain on an empty playing field   water from out of the clouds

individual sequences and poems   who and what I once was
tomatoes ripening in autumn sun   not definitive, incomplete
a question about interpretation   the reader co-creates
making better choices   trying to find the time
impatient and impetuous   not into end of line rhyme
invasion as noble effort   corresponding with all my friends

japanese maple in autumn sun   moment in the mind
turn from the sleeping woman   she is not looking at me
scrutiny and interrogation   emerging from the self
sensuous level of perception   wild laugh of relief
face lit up softly sheds the years   emotions without cause
current theories of the mind   I am trying to get home

knots have long figured in magic   ties us all to the mast
strings and magnets and clockwork   like the back of my hand
we don't live near heaven   knowledge blinks out of view
question the nature of music   sound engulfs the room
low light leaking from metaphor   signal fading then gone
it is all there so to speak   faith structures defeating the eye

lots to interest and entertain   things we've all heard about
limited time high turnaround   repeated fractures and breaks
frequent loud interruptions   someone has something to say
start out with different intentions   in isolation now
at the centre of the story   said I looked like her son
long way to go for transcendence   my whole being shakes

mirror, inkblot, shadow, chair   puzzles of different shapes
two simple loops the very same size   drawings made out of names
complete or partial anagrams   a hundred empty rooms
rejection through the letterbox   interrupted plans
always intense and personal   a huge amount of work
names have a special significance   it's time to leave the stage

nothing less than everything   private self and public world
training as a visionary   cheap teenage punks with guns
medium of transformation   the touch of a dead man's hand
history requires that fear   made several attempts to speak
words lost through coastal erosion   rethinking the time
an occasion to see beyond this   nowhere in her eyes

over the hills and far away   music played till dawn
end of the world flickers into view   stretching from earth to sky
chronological familiarity   no time left to spare
overwhelming restlessness   destination made quite clear
structure is now cellular   a circle of events
closed eyes see the mirror   the magic morning is here

prayer flags strung out in the wind   mountains in the mist
the future stood around to view   moments undefined
repeated rites of passage   life cycles built for one
debris from exploded buddhas   caves in which to hide our souls
hummingbird returns to me   frozen in mid-air
summoning angels to quiz them   phrases older than rhyme

questions to be answered   dead husband in her dreams
apple and orange on three sticks   spring greenery and flowers
evil eye and borrowed pail   speak ill of absent friends
never struck by lightning   burnt with a blue flame
straw torches or small bonfires   what we have never seen
all things turn and spin and change   restlessness resumes

representation of temporal aspects   their morale was intact
someone will get it into their head   the intercom might have failed
down the lane past the houses   the sheer chaos that war brings
blear-eyed google and squinting   makes physical demands
draw the same line down the canvas   trample corn to pick the flowers
self-disgust and unvoiced rage   out of the house for hours

sunflower waiting to bud in September   a kind of refining move
specialisation producing restlessness   the next turn on the right
try and upset our way of seeing   digital photographs and film
doodles on small bits of paper   blown up very large
my office is a dining table   parent to all these words
fifteen squares in a dark tunnel   reports from another world

trying to write an alphabet with sand   in a busy rush-hour street
a city of the future   got everything it should
twisted circles make a chain   be sure that it's complete
writing an imaginary letter   words glued to a sign
hang a string across the room   photocopy the world outside
ask to be buried out of doors   where the dead and living join

unanimity of opinion   only increases mystique
this thing could peel a planet   a crescendo of yells and leaps
slowly squeezed out of the picture   shabby symbols of life
large slabs of polished black granite   heads studying the floor
derangement of the senses   looking filthy and sad
further riots would follow   spearheading the new sound

versions of songs with similar tunes   another burnt-out old ruin
a kind of recuperation at work   this piece not conceptual at all
pointing hissing and stamping   next morning blind in one eye
real things were distant   reason a weathered stone
surprise blurred by vibration   everything in the shade
biting their thin bony knuckles   threshold of heaven and earth

we have known adjustment   illustrated tomes
collaborated together   working in various styles
often a good balance to be found   visions of magic and string
intelligence taste and feeling   known for disturbing the peace
hoping to receive an answer   hands and arms above the head
do not doubt in asking   futile gestures and signs

x marked on the treasure map   information is unique
people want us to have attitude   start unloading the van
invisible drawings in whiteness   we'll never work again
barely noticeable atmosphere   sound obscured and transformed
unbroken skin emits a high pitch   drowning in its own tune
prayer and liturgical activity   always looking down

yes the moon is full tonight   planning may take three years
open space is the best use of land   treasured and lucky ground
ecological concerns have been voiced   tidal marshes must be filled
leaves only when he chooses   stones in his or her hand
timber platform or extension   dangerous starlight and dreams
a call to prayer for the living   spirits gather as well

z what we use to symbolize snores   constant access to the noise
little stabs of happiness   smiles reflected in other's frowns
retire and live in lofty seclusion   two feet dragging slow
surface rather than chamber   unmuscled as a child
a recording of past and specific place   neither human nor machine
a far away hum of voices   beautiful as last night's dream

GORDON KENNEDY
venice

city, construct, kinematograph
    gold hive of intrigue & decay
        its mouths concealed by fans

in mirrors hid in mirrors
    from a play of eyes & faces
        desperate with festival

conjurors & jugglers
    tradesmen, courtesans
        smashed clowns in silhouette

bright carnival masks implicit
    with the gestures of our watchmakers
        their shadows on the arches

hands whose charmed creations frame
    cut slits where eyes reflect
        the formal game

in streetless adjectival
    moon: one oar-slit
        flux down soundlessly

assumed canals' convergence
    on the hidden garden
        at the city's heart

where terraced fountains
    arc the moonlit
        open rose

condensing in that
    first red mouth:
        a drop of single dew

reflecting in that
    curvature
        this

the guild of surgical alchemists

the work begins with her acceptance of a gift

an inexpensive watch perhaps
some poor example of a tool of her profession
which she will not recognise as secondhand

she arrives at the time appointed
(no: she comes there late)

in the former medical wing
of the halmstad university
(yes: the original building)

she had been reading

in the state of organised revolt
conformity becomes the only true rebellion

she arrives in time
& now is moving through the corridors

the doors here are perceptual
impossible to walk through

a door is opened to reveal a door behind

eventually there is a door made out of wood
she stands in front now
looking through the small square hole

behind the hole
a piece of paper, moving
right left down up
scratching, rustling

on the paper words & numbers
some of which are legible

:

at one point the phrase *pful gui*
passes briefly across the opening

beside the square hole is a piece of string
weighted by a pencil

with which she is perhaps expected
to write on the moving paper:
there is the implication of mathematics

at one point, on the surface is written
the birds of paper will not fly alone

some of the letters
do not look like letters

she cannot work the machine of paper & pencil:
another attempt is permitted
but the question has changed now, subtly

:

in the inner room she finds them waiting
disposed around the space in ones
all standing sitting patiently fingering the artefacts
each of them attending at a different junction
in the narrative

some carry unsheathed implements, as symbols

see we have collected all historic instruments
in maintenance of what is past
museum we are hospital are gallery

(brief extract from the physical catalogue
one manual of handwashing techniques
one porcelain sink, excessive pitted
one gas mask
one glass syringe)

do not suppose, however, we are antiquarians:
the adept holds to both the inner
& the outer work

ah we are practical men

this room that we are in
may be a text, some work of visual art
& yet you will agree, bears all
the outward hallmarks of a game

:

her eyes adapt

the room fills up with flasks & papers
instruments of surgery & language
charts, leaves, tapestries

her eye is drawn towards a quote
with a single error only
stripping apparent surfaces away
& revealing the infinite which was hid

& when she looks there is a wooden table
when she looks there is a mound of shavings on the wood
& when she looks the mound is the size of anatomy

& they are sweeping the shavings to the floor

when what is underneath is fully visible they stop
& in her hand an instrument appears

from somewhere a hand points to an eye
from nowhere a hand points to a heart
giving the impression of choice
where there is no choice

(the heart is opened to reveal an eye
the eye is opened to reveal a heart)

o corpus gloriosum
body academic

ah one body now

SARAH LAW

Prynne Knows My Name

It hangs like a calligraphic hinge
within the recesses. Dark and astigmatic,
the act of naming shivers a release. In
with the pin-prick of a chance; informal
splicing of regality, contextualising knowledge.

It is the fuming of a censor swung through
the plunge of agnosticism. Counting the slow
beats of a carpet song. Clinging, my difference
to the black jacket of singular stance, against
all laws of residual shlock (and the hourly glance).

He knows the counterblast of appetite.
Slops on the directory causing stuck words,
lost chronicles dashed with young blood,
lung flood, and a small white scroll issued
with aplomb. Script-lash is more than enough.

Death of a Visionary

It was the habit of her small, gnarled hands
to say the beads, to tell them daily
how through the freeze frame of a child's fingers,
a plethora of mothers found their forms. That woman
was as real as the dirt that bit their feet,
Lucia and the ragged siblings with her,
dirt they had no word for. Then that light:
a gold-edged spectrum in a dirt-poor night
and a voice that couldn't be heard. Only
her rose-lipped smile, her open palms,
snow white, vulnerable. In her face
such sorrow for the mud-stained human race.
The rest was fragile, intricate, like lace
for priests to press and sisters to unravel.

To see these things and live: that was her sentence.
The fragile wish of her bones for severance
tapped at whispers threaded together;
rumours of war. Fear. Rough cloth at the wrist.
A vision of the ministry of silence, bright
and overexposed. And finished. And much missed.

Meditation Topics for Women

1. If a bird wishes to join the sisters for meditation, but can't follow the office hymns, what is one to do?

2. If there are twelve sisters presently resident, why do there sometimes seem twice this many at 5pm meditation?

3. If a sister should suddenly seem drunk and eager to sit only in sunshine, should this be permitted?

4. If one suspects a sister has red wine in her cell, should one visit her in the hope of being offered a glass?

5. If the slim tabby cat wishes to join the sisters and the bird for meditation, where should she sit?

6. If the mother superior offers each of the sisters a small wildflower from the grounds, is it customary to offer one back?

7. Should the statue of Our Lady cry, which sister should offer an apology?

8. If a sister should levitate, is it prudent to take photographs?

9. Should a priest vanish at the altar, must cleaning be postponed?

10. How many sisters does it take to change an altar cloth?

11. How many suppers does it take to fill a sister's bones with health?

12. How many palm crosses does it take to build a workable two-sister raft?

GILES GOODLAND

Thought Experiments

I

the words are deciding the next
there's nothing less real than its word
nothing changes things like light
a change is a chance gone solid
a tissue of chances makes a person
a person is a mixture of rain
rain disintegrated before our eyes
last night's dream is today's rain
we joined an association of dreams
shape is the association of memory
each shape hinges a variant world
mist is the shape of language
we have a hazy idea of mist
mist tries to break through
each word is a potential break
words rust on the sword of history
history started with the full-stop
a full-stop is longer than a sentence
everyone invents one sentence
no sentence should be thought
fire is the thought of matter
thought is as bodily as taking a shit
a mind is a body of language
the machine in my mouth ran language
a machine sleeps in a closed book
sleep continues work by other means
the alarm clock cried itself to sleep
folk-songs are the cries of dead labourers
dead objects outnumber the living
flowers believe themselves into life
time flowers on wallpaper
concrete is sand in time's hands
time is the root of the poem
the longest poem is is

nowhere is the capital of nothing
nothing adheres like a road
roads carry blood into the city
a city is as old as its name
desire is a name for forgetfulness
birds convert desire to sound
a bird lands on its shadow
people are shadows that places cast
I do not accept that that
I'll be ready for the end of the sentence
before the sentence language was endless
those the language names are guilty
language connects like a fist
I can connect shadow with shadow
someone kept watering the shadow
the field shook off its suit of water
water is superfluous dream
life is the dream of the inanimate
that dream is incorrect
corrections were listed in the hedgerow
the moon showed me a list of the moon
streetlights show through my skin
skin is a readjustment of dust
dust is the secretion of time
time has too many syllables
each syllable says it is a word
words thumbprint the mountain
this is now the word for something else
words run a ring around trees
a book is a tree's foreknowledge
a mind rushed like a tree in a breeze
a frame of mind has no window
a window believes in ghosts
there was a belief in the air in the air
at night stars believe in themselves
nights buckle under media pressure
the night cracks under the door
the door opens under its word
the words are deciding.

II

oil blooms under hills. Birds seep into dark

time is your pulse. Its glassy face is yours

mud incorporates under the path. These horses in their fields of
yellow stars are of us

remember history. It was the softening of pears in a bowl

objects of desire change but not desire. The light turned off not the
switch

you commit good acts unconsciously and evil acts consciously. The
more aware we are the worse

a car adds moving colours to the landscape. Happiness is an effect of
serotonin

you distort the answer by posing the question. There is a hole in the
floor of the sentence

the boot into the skull. The word into the head

death has the shape of conception's instant. The sperm entombs
himself

but that dream was incorrect. I should have dreamt

novels denser than Finnegans Wake. But I have never remembered
more than

another morning. Could this grey really be the most contemporary
moment yet

god loves a thought. Each one fills the void slightly more

puddles have oceans. Shadows have nights

superseded. Footways seed like vestigial parts of consciousness

later I am driving. I come to a splendid house where

the subject cancels the future. I is the delete command

worse than entropy is its reverse. No voice dissipating to

it will begin. It ended

III

a hoverfly is a single bead on an invisible abacus

the river is slipping from the word river

the ignorance of bliss is so profound we can't tell who woke the
neighbours

philosophy is using last week's TV guide to tell you what's on tonight

sleep is spending some small time without illusion

language is a virus asking all sufferers to record their impressions

a river is a machine for parting light from reflection

sky's reply to earth is moderated by earth's knowledge of ocean

perception is relative to ice melting on mountains

at oceanic depth the congealing of stone is relative to perception

the foetus is a complete deity whose universe is timeless

time is woven into your clothes but you cannot trace it to meet your skin

brain is a limb that can grab a galaxy and particularize the mote

the equilibrium of night is maintained through the cries of animals

the reason we don't remember most dreams is most are untranslatable

self is a multiple occupant of the same shell over time

the thought of hardness is a substance to push

a judgement is continuously being made in my absence.

SPENCER SELBY

Barbecue

Little remove I straddle
as prehensile limb took

initiative with my own
nationwide guarantee

Took gross tonnage by merit
suspended from price index

atavistic junkyard satellite
transmitting code announcing

that fifty years of pollution
is career enough to retire early

How else rate service when
the best oxygen has gone away

Little remove I straddle
by choice of lawn furniture

stained with catsup and blood
in equal parts I can't tell apart

Creature comfort divine
on the grill but doesn't

see the value daylight
never takes for granted

It's luxury I do covet
in defense here now

of a faded frontier cushion
with gravy on the side

Nocturne

Once they were dim pockets
frayed and brittle arms
during the souvenir invasion

homesick for anything
beating softly in the firmament

in the murky glare of glass
in narcotic waves over the desert

as a child later than this
smear of trajectory
from dome car passage

would take endurance
and suddenly I'm awake

and beside me is a reason
to keep going back

Social Comment

Screams compete
with open windows
in this part of town

Outlets dominate
that carry camouflage
as far as the eye can see

So alike and only
thinking of one thing
we have to do

A single danger to avoid
reason to ignore

perfect light
at the start
absorbing what is true

JOHN SEED

from Pictures from Mayhew – London 1850

XXXII

1

The poor people who supply me
with rats are what you may
call barn-door labouring poor for
they are the most ignorant people I
ever come near really you would
not believe people could live in
such ignorance talk about Latin &
Greek sir why English is Latin
to them in fact I have
a difficulty to understand them myself

2

when the harvest is got in
they go hunting the hedges &
ditches for rats
once the farmers had to pay
2*d.* a-head for all rats
caught on their grounds
& they nailed them
up against the wall but now
the rat-ketchers can get 3*d.* each
by bringing the vermin up to town the farmers
don't pay them anything
to hunt them in their stacks & barns
they no longer get their 2*d.* in the country
though they get their 3*d.* in town

3

there is a wonderful deal of difference
in the specie of rats
the bite of sewer
or waterditch rats is
very bad their
coats is poisonous the water
& ditch rat lives on filth
but your barn-rat is a plump fellow
& he lives on the best of everything he's
well off
there's as much difference
between the barn & sewer-rats
as between a brewer's horse & a costermonger's

4

Rats want a deal of watching
& a deal of sorting now you
can't put a sewer & a
barn-rat together it's like
putting a Roosshian & a Turk
under the same roof I can tell
a barn-rat from a ship-rat
or a sewer-rat in a minute
there's six or seven different kinds of rats
& if we don't sort 'em they
tear one another to pieces

5

A rat's bite is very singular
it's a three-cornered one like a leech's
only deeper of course
& it will bleed for
ever such a time my boys

have sometimes had their fingers
go dreadfully bad from rat-bites
all black & putrid like
aye as black as the horse-hair covering to my sofa
people have said to me you
ought to send the lad to the hospital
& have his finger took off but
I've always left it to the lads
& they've said oh
don't mind it father
it'll get all right by & by &
so it has

6
The best thing I
ever found for a rat-bite
was the thick bottoms of
porter casks
put on as a poultice the
only thing you can do is to poultice
these porter bottoms is so powerful
& draws so
they'll take thorns out of horses' hoofs & feet
after steeplechasing

GASTÓN BAQUERO

translated by Mark Weiss

Marcel Proust Cruises The Bay Of Corinth *

Each day old Anaximander
sat beneath the shade of youth in flower.
The famous sage had grown so old
that his lips no longer parted, nor did he smile nor seem even to
    understand
the play of golden hair the laughter, the sly, flirtatious games
of the loveliest girls in Corinth.

It was towards the end of his life,
when as he passed folk would comment
that there was left to him at most
the wilting of three or four sunflowers,
it was in that small morsel of time preceding death,
that Anaximander discovered
the solution to the enigma of time.

There, in Corinth, by the bay, encircled by the flowering girls.
That he would shelter at noon beneath a green and blue parasol had
    been accepted
as a harmless eccentricity.
He had ceased greeting his age-mates, he no longer frequented the
    places where the old would gather,
nor did he seem to share with those in the agora
anything other than years and the snow encircling their jaws:
    Anaximander
would sit, mute, in the time of flowering youth,
like one who goes abroad to cure an old illness.

It began at noon in the sonorous shade of the girls of Corinth;
impassive, his parasol open, he dragged his feet to where he would sit
    in silence,
to where he would seat himself among them, listening to their cooing,
    observing the delicate geometry of knees the color of wheat,
    glancing furtively at those fugitive pink doves
that flew beneath the bridge of shoulders.

He said nothing,
and nothing seemed to stir him beneath his parasol, sensing, among
        the sweet girls of Corinth, time's passage, time become a
        shower
of golden pins, resplendent as ripe cherries,
time flowing around the ankles of the flowering doves of Corinth,
time, which in other places brings to the lips of men a draught of
        poison which none may turn away,
here offered the nectar of an ambrosia so singular
one would have thought that time itself wished also to live, to become
        incarnate, to delight
in smooth skin or in the reflection of a blue-green eye.
                                        Silently Anaximander
floated like a swan each day between clouds of beauty, and endured;
there, within time and beyond it, he tasted the slow fragrance of
        eternity, while his cat purred beside the fire. At evening he
        would return home
and pass the night writing tiny poems
for the noisy doves of Corinth.

The city's other sages muttered ceaselessly.
More even than the harvest festival or the comings and goings of ships,
        Anaximander had become
the preferred topic of tiresome conversations:
                                "Always have I told you,
wise men of Corinth," his old enemy Prodicos proclaimed, "that he
        was no true sage nor even of average importance. His work?
Plagiarized. Repetitious. And hollow at the core. Hollow as a barrel of
        wine after the Thebans have come to taste the sunlight of
        Corinthian vineyards."
Impassive, Anaximander walked through the streets of Corinth to the bay,
his blue parasol open above him, catching the latest news in passing:
day after day some wise old man would pass below. Day after day the
        sages
would be summoned by Proserpina, their ashes only
flowing towards the sea, the violet-covered waters of the sea at Corinth.

All passed, and Anaximander remained, encircled by the girls, seated
        beneath the sun.
A fold of Atalanta's blouse, Aglae's voice

when she sang to the heavens her hymn in imitation of the nightingale,
Anadiomena's smile, were all the sustenance Anaximander needed,
    and he was there, still there, when everything around him had
    vanished.

One day he saw in the distance
a small boat on the horizon of the Bay of Corinth.
Within, a little man rowed with an asthmatic's exhausted tenacity.
His head was covered with a straw hat, a white straw hat with a red band.
    From its confines
the little man looked out upon the entire bay and saw, on its furthest
    shore,
a blue parasol, a small circle as golden as the sun. He rowed
towards it. Stubborn, tenacious, whistling a tune, the little man with
    gloved hands
rowed ceaselessly. Anaximander began to smile. The boat, immobile
    on the bay,
had also conquered time. Slowly the white straw hat announced that
    the little man was receding into the distance homeward.

                        That night, shortly before retiring,
Marcel Proust, exhilarated, called from his home:
"Mother, bring me more paper, bring me all the paper you can.
I'm going to begin a new chapter. I'm going to call it
"In the Shade of the Flowering Girls."

* The poem is structured around the title of the second volume of Proust's
Remembrance of Things Past, *A l'ombre des jeunes filles en fleur*, called in the
standard English translation *Within a Budding Grove*.

Count Cagliostro's Cat

I had a cat named Tamerlaine.
And all it ate were poems by Emily Dickinson
and Schubert melodies.

He traveled with me: in Paris
they served him on lace doilies
chocolate confections made for him and him alone
by Madame de Sevigné herself.
To no avail: he waved them off
like a Roman emperor
presiding over a night of orgies.

Page by page, verse by verse,
he wished only to chew on
old editions of Emily Dickinson's poems
and he listened incessantly
to Schubert melodies.

(In Munich, in a German pension, we met
Katherine Mansfield, and she,
who held within her all the world's
delicacy, for Tamerlaine played sweetly on her cello
Schubert melodies).

Tamerlaine passed away in the most appropriate manner:
we were on our way through Amsterdam, through the ghetto, to be exact,
and as we passed the front of the oldest synagogue
Tamerlaine stopped, looked at me with all love's splendor in his eyes
and leaped into the interior of a dark temple.

Since then, each year,
I send a bunch of poems as a present to the old
synagogue of Amsterdam.
                              Poems that were wept one day in Amherst
by Emily, that melancholy lady,
Emily Tamerlaine Dickinson.

Charada For Lydia Cabrera

One horse, two butterfly, three sailor,
look at the horse, look at the sailor,
look at the butterfly.
The sailor is dressed in white
the horse's hide is white,
the white butterfly laughs.
Three sailor, two butterfly, one horse,
the sailor flies over the white horse,
the butterfly over the sailor,
two butterfly, one horse, three sailor,
the horse looks at the butterfly,
the sailor looks at his horse's white laughter,
the butterfly looks at the sailor, looks at the horse,
the horse flies, the sailor sings
the butterfly a lullaby,
the horse sleeps and dreams of the sailor,
the butterfly sleeps and dreams it's the horse,
the sailor sleeps and dreams of becoming a butterfly,
one horse, two butterfly, three sailor,
three butterfly, two sailor, one horse,
one sailor, one horse, one butterfly.

ALBERTO BLANCO

translated by Joan Lindgren

Micas

1

My house is no different
from the pages of a book

Its name reminds me
of a cage and of dawn

Slowly my house
was constructed by night
nights of an industrious dream
my father's
habitual dream

And there where it was established
it will be established once more

Because my house
was a long
slow time being built and
according to the ancient thesis

That the ends go out from
and return to the means

2

Under the mine
and above the heat
there lies my house

My house of mica
went on growing smaller
the way the years
were peeling away

the branches of copper
from their tree of levy

And the wise candlestick
that burned in the night
had to adjust itself
to the transparency
of uncertainty

Since then my house
is an open window
an interior landscape
that light has made
with the iron soul
of a handful of coins

Limestone

I

Barefoot at times
at other times shod
pearl without shell
shell without pearl

Silent at times
other times rowdy
as if ready
to take over the sky

Whether life appear
and as suddenly dissolve
like a stratagem

The light of limestone
can outdo the sum
of our celebrations

2

The majority of bones
lying scattered in the earth
are greatly in limestone's debt

Either for metamorphosis
for the resurrection of metals
or for the omnipresence of death

Sandstone

Landscape
and eyes
are one

Sand
and desert
are one

Heart
and witness
are one

They are an
ever eroding sign
which says

"No quantity
can exceed
the sky"–

Basalt

There where the caravans
of an undersea desert
remember having seen
a countercurrent

Nomad stones have fished
with common nets
in watery currents
having asked permission of no one –

Tezontle

According to the untrustworthy
slopes of both good and bad
etymologies

We might say
that the name 'tezontle'

Has something to do
with two-colored mirrors

Something to do
with the eyes of the volcanoes

Something to do
with the potter's song

And something as well with
the glyphs of abysses

Granite

In that place where
spring's green stars
set up a bazar
upon the steppe

Facing the archipelago
a gray mare dwells
adored by the clouds,
whose backs are turned to the sky

ROBERT WALSER

translated by Christopher Middleton

To Georg Trakl

In a foreign country I might be reading you
or just as well at home
and your verses were a pleasure to me always;
definitely in the room
round me the radiance, the shimmer
of marvellous expressions you had found,
never once was any thought of mine forlorn.
A clinging mantle seemed to clothe me
there, in the abyss of reading,
intent upon the beauty of your being,
which is the swan, the boat, the garden
and atmospheres they too dispense
as up they float, you, opulent
with leaves, ineffably sould, lissome oak,
tumbled rock, whisk of a moose's tail,
a little girl, her dancing, yours, dejected ginat,
here on a meadow in the Jura where
in play, as if I dreamed it, I propose
this address to your genius.
Did some perpetuation of the fate
of Hölderlin reverberate around your cradle
and keeping you company, as life went on,
doom you at last to golden lunacy?
Your poems, when I read them, more and more
carry me away as in a splendid coach and four.

Rilke

In a lonely château
not long ago
somewhat of an exile
on the horse anent Pegasus
you rode, rather serious,
with seldom a smile
in landscapes of mood
that flashed and glowed
you strove for the truth
of importunate Youth.
Hard for the Poem you fought.
Now be at peace, adorn,
shimmering fruit
in a shapely bowl,
the lyric pavilion.
Unruffled repose,
when duty is done
and off you shake,
each by each,
life's travelling shoes,
is beauty enough.
I was content to make
beside your grave
this little speech.

January 4, 1927

Sentiment

Whatever it was in plain sight
gave me fresh heart, if, nonetheless
it could not, being nature, give me rest,
soon it will be far away, outside.

I'll go without it then, this glow,
this ringing of the sounds and of the colours,
and with a passion sing of it. Somehow, as if
what's missing left me with a mystery,
its absence make me love it all twice over.

Once you have seen it with your inward eye,
a beautiful thing spreads beauty all around
To dote on it, or want it back again, is wrong.
It walks along with you, kept well in mind.

October, 1927

Pascin

A little prudish, a little crude
his drawings are mostly of comical things,
I mean that the line his pencil has spent
is dainty, but also impudent.
I own a picture of his: the maid
told me to hide it from her sight.
On Potsdamerstrasse, in the glow
from a musical cabaret's window,
our two persons met one night.
We talked in whispers for a while.
As I walked home, I saw a crew
of workmen still with work to do.
Sometimes his pictures,
combining nasty things with nice,
have attracted critics' strictures.
Divinely Lukas Cranach could
portray his nudities naive
and naturally dignified.
You certainly will run a risk
when daintiness makes you a prude;
so we walk on and our hurts frisk
like puppydoggies at our side.

PETER HUCHEL

translated by Harry Guest

Under the Constellation of Hercules

Somewhere
no bigger
than the circle
a hawk might trace
on the sky at dusk.

A wall rough-
hewn burnt
by reddish moss.
A distant bell conveying
the smoke of olive-trees
over shimmering water.
Fire
fed by straw
and damp foliage
filtered by voices
you don't recognise.

Submitting to the night
to its icy harness
Hercules draws the chain-
harrow of stars
up the northern sky.

LUTZ SEILER   *Two Poems*
            translated by Tony Frazer

my vintage, sixty-three, that

            endless stream of children, fastened
to the halls' echo-vault, creeping
along stooped into some-

one else's coat pocket, seven
    full of wax with a heavy weight exhaled
by hallways, eight

        with a weight that rose
to the head from bowls of piss, we had
        gagarin, but then gagarin

had us, every morning the same, writing
followed by scratching sleeves
across desks and at midday
spoons striking the hour, we had

table duty, milk duty, the pressure
    of a void in our eyes jelly
        in our ears until
it fell silent
gravity fell silent
        in our caps
        those were the pains

while peeing, in the barrier wood
while talking, we had
quotations: that at least we *were holding out a light*
        to the dark side of the planet
            first all together & then
                each of us once more
                quietly to himself, we had

no luck. so the houses collapse
            finally we become
        small again &
ride back into the villages built of wood, built
of straw, that we came from, full of cracks, thin
with an echo sharpened

on the wind: we greet Gagarin, we
had no luck, back down, back
to our villages
            & away from the villages
over the fields at night . . .

                              ****

we lay off madagascar and had[1]

                                    lost
the world and the point: we lay
    off gera, off krossen, we trained
the roots, revolution from below, not
bismarck, lenin, insects
came in, smaller
    than their sounds; yet our hands
leaned damp and heavy before us
on the ocean banks, half

forgotten the prayer lay
    below, the campaign chest
deeper still, prehistoric aluminum
loaves, above them

copied space, copied air: four
polish tank crew and a simple
dog, invincible in its fear and at night
    the clicking of its claws
        never-ending, doglike, unbeaten ... something

these places didn't lose, they had
lost everything: that
it had happened there – the axe handle
in the head, the club foot, the boiler room behind
the redskins' spinney, where we
tortured *the slaves*, first nitzold, then
   stöcklein, just
like *the seawolf*, episode 3; we had
the plague on board, at 6 a.m. desolation standing
on the steps outside with the most sensitive soles,
waiting; thus it was we went

out early every morning so
overshadowed by our own thoughts
lost in dreamland disguised
as fear in the belladonna bush and as sweetness
   in the flowering nettles – wasn't
the path clamped to us, waving there
at the edge of the path? to the traces

of script, the black marks remaining on the gate, to
stöcklein in his hammock, that
   splintering blow to his
face, air-sounds, in the mist, did they say
gravity reverses *in the mist* ?

stöcklein is dead and nitzold
has the mangle. only we
   still look
a mess, we sing,
we spring up a song forgotten halfway up our throats
and our lunch bags whirl on their straps
like madagascan coyotes around our necks

---

[1] The title quotes a famous German song, "Wir lagen vor Madagaskar und hatten
die Pest an Bord" (*We lay off Madagascar and had the plague on board*. See http://
ingeb.org/Lieder/wirlage2.mid where there is a good digital version of the melody.
The song was written by Just Scheu (1903-1956), actor, composer and dramatist.

ANJA UTLER

translated by Tony Frazer

sibyl – poem in eight syllables

> *Сивилла: выжжена, сивилла: ствол.*
> *Все птицы вымерли, но Бог вошел.*
>
> *Sibyl: burned out, Sibyl: the trunk.*
> *All the birds perished, but God came in.*

has touched the: spores, bare-eyed: bared mouth is in-
flamed, sibyl, she shudders, glows: sand singes the tips the
finger the tongue strikes sparks in her body: blazes up

*

she: sways, sibyl, slave to slithering sands she rushes, streams
— myriad pores — she wafts away she flashes across the sun — becomes:
sunstorm — murmurs she spits, knows: she no longer subsides

*

is: burst, sibyl, the: sliver in the flesh she is — still bleeding? —
splinters — sundered, gaping: like the lips, stem — is: gills, lignified
she: splits the light, drips: she rasps, that: shoots up

*

sibyl thus: she yawns, groans: oscillating the: vocal folds, glottal gaps they
scratch: away over the chalk, scouring, rending a: crater from
hip to throat the: gullet, sibyl, she: trembles, vibrates

*

vibrates, is: the quivering, sibyl — tremor — twitches: in swirling sand in
whirling winds she grinds abandoned: the joint sprained, whimpers: to
the strip: she is consumed — trembles: uprooted pines — she: erodes

*

sibyl she: towers up, turns into: cliffs she sizzles is the: spray in the
pores dies away she radiates: sibilants, dissolves – sss – ebbs
floods herself and: sighs

*

she: staggers, sibyl she: breaks up in whirling heat she: sizzles
whistles: swamp, pond slippery thighs the: reed belt soaks she sur-
rounds herself gurgles — adder — slips away in: susurrus

*

*

and silent, just the scent: burned soil clearing perceptible – is
past crackling – and decay: toes finger the stalk:
a mulch hollow, poking the thrown-off skin: crumbles
down to flaking soles and: starts rustling

Notes on Contributors

GASTÓN BAQUERO was born in Banes, Cuba, in 1918 and died in Madrid in 1997. A child of rural poverty, Baquero trained as an agronomist, earning a doctorate in Natural Sciences from the University of Havana before turning to a career in journalism and literature. He was a founder or collaborated on all of the most important Cuban literary journals of the 30, 40s and 50s, including *Orígenes*. As an editor, journalist and essayist he worked for several newspapers and journals closely connected to the Batista regime, and he left Cuba immediately after the revolution, spending the rest of his life in Spain. Thereafter he was officially nonexistent in Cuba, unpublished there and written out of the history of Cuban poetry. His poetry, including the work published after he left, was nonetheless widely known to poets on the island. In the last decade he has been "rehabilitated," and is once more publicly acknowledged as one of Cuba's major poets. A bilingual selection of his poems, translated by Mark Weiss, will appear eventually. Baquero published numerous essays and eight collections of poetry. The present selection is drawn from *Magias e invenciones* (Ediciones Cultura Hispanica, Madrid, 1984).

ALBERTO BLANCO's poems in this issue are drawn from *El libro de las piedras* (The Book of Stones), published in Mexico City by Conaculta in 2003. Born in Mexico City in 1951, he is the author of over twenty books of poetry, short stories and children's books. His Selected Poems in English translation appeared in 1995 from City Lights, San Francisco, under the title *Dawn of the Senses*. He is also a musician.

TONY FRAZER is editor of *Shearsman* and publisher of Shearsman Books. The translation of Anja Utler's *sibyl* was prepared for the poet's first UK reading at the CCCP event in Cambridge, April 2005, and the versions of Lutz Seiler's poems were prepared for the poet's appearance at the Sydney Writers' Festival in May 2005. The epigraph in Anja Utler's poem was translated by Belinda Cooke.

GILES GOODLAND's last book was *A Spy in the House of Years* (Leviathan, 2001), a digest of the 20th century in 100 parts, with one for each year. He lives in London and works as a lexicographer.

HARRY GUEST was born in Wales in 1932 and lives in Exeter with his wife, Lynn Guest, a historical novelist. His *Collected Poems 1955-2000*, titled *A Puzzling Harvest*, appeared from Anvil in 2002.

GAD HOLLANDER lives in London. His books include *Walserian Waltzes*, *Benching With Virgil* (both from Avec Books, Penngrove, CA 2000) and *The Palaver*, a collaborative artist's book with Andrew Bick (Book Works, London 1998). His films & videos include "Euripides' Movies" (1987), "Diary of Sane

Man" (1990), "the palaver transcription" (2000) and "Talker" (2003). *Theatre of Psychodialysis* is a work in progress and regress, an oscillating labour with no fixed abode, its projected form suspended like the redundant ampersand in black & white. Special thanks to translator and poet Cristina Viti for the cut-up of *The Palaver* that became the opening section of *Black Love*, and for collaborating on the text's final edit.

PETER HUCHEL was one of the major figures in post-war German poetry, and died in 1983. Anvil has published a fine collection of his work in Michael Hamburger's translation under the title *The Garden of Theophrastus*.

PHILIP JENKINS lives in Cardiff. His publications include *On the Beach with Eugène Boudin* (Transgravity Press, Deal, 1978), *Cairo* (Books 1 and 2 — Editions Grand Hôtel de Palme à Palerme, London, 1981) and *Travels with Kandy* (short fiction — Rigmarole Books, Melbourne, 1982). The third part of *Cairo* appears here for the first time. Parts 1 and 2 can be most easily found in the anthology *A State of Independence*, ed. Tony Frazer (Stride Publications, Exeter, 1998), which is still in print.

GORDON KENNEDY is a writer and an electronic/improv musician who lives in Glasgow. Recent work of his has appeared in *Fire, Poetry Review* and *The Rialto*. During 2005 he plans to become someone else for the year, and film the results. www.organica.co.uk

SARAH LAW studied literature at Cambridge and London universities. She currently teaches literature and creative writing at UEA, Norwich. She has two poetry collections published by Stride (*Bliss Tangle*, 1999, *The Lady Chapel*, 2003). She lives in Norwich and is interested in the links between spirituality, art and writing. The poems here are drawn from a new collection called *Perihelion*, which Shearsman Books will publish in 2006.

JOAN LINDGREN is a Fulbright Border Scholar, and lives on the US/Mexican Border. *Unthinkable Tenderness: Selected Poems of Juan Gelman*, which she edited and translated, was published by the University of California Press in 1997. Her translations of Alberto Blanco appeared in the anthology *Reversible Monuments* (Copper Canyon Press, 2003) and in various literary journals including *Modern Poetry in Translation*. An anthology of Spanish poets is currently under consideration for publication.

RUPERT M. LOYDELL is Managing Editor of the Exeter-based publishing house Stride and the web magazine *Stride* (www.stridemagazine.co.uk). His most recent collection, *A Conference of Voices*, was published by Shearsman in October 2004.

CHRISTOPHER MIDDLETON should need no introduction to readers of this magazine. He is one of Britain's finest living poets and a pioneering translator of German poetry. His latest collection of poems is *The Anti-Basilisk*, due for publication shortly at Sheep Meadow Press in the USA and, in the autumn of 2005, at Carcanet Press, Manchester. Shearsman Books published his *Palavers, and a Nocturnal Journal* (consisting of a long interview and a journal) in September 2004.

FRANCES PRESLEY's latest collection is the excellent *Paravane. New and Selected Poems* from Salt Publishing, Cambridge (2004). She lives in London and is a member of the editorial board of *How2*. The four poems here are drawn from a long sequence called *Myne*.

LISA SAMUELS is the author of *LETTERS, The Seven Voices, War Holdings* and, most recently, *Paradise for Everyone*, published by Shearsman Books in April 2005 and from which these three poems are drawn. In addition to poetry, she has published work on modernist and contemporary writers, intellectual property in the humanities, and critical practices. She currently teaches at the University of Wisconsin-Milwaukee.

SAM SAMPSON here makes his third appearance in Shearsman. He grew up in West Auckland, New Zealand, and attended Auckland University, where he majored in Philosophy and taught Ethnomusicology. His poems have appeared in *Ariel, Landfall, Slope, Stand, NZ Listener, Poetry Review, Jacket* and *Salt*.

ROBERT SAXTON makes his second *Shearsman* appearance in this issue. He was born in Nottingham in 1952, and now lives in north London, where he is the editorial director of an illustrated-book publishing company. He has published two collections: *The Promise Clinic* (Enitharmon Press, London, 1994) and *Manganese* (Carcanet Press, Manchester, 2003).

JOHN SEED was born in the North-East of England, but now lives in London, and teaches History at Roehampton University. Shearsman Books published two volumes of his work in April 2005: *New and Collected Poems* & *Pictures from Mayhew*, from the latter of which the poems here are drawn. Every single word of these poems is drawn from Henry Mayhew's mid-19th century reports of the condition of the London poor. John Seed has taken the transcriptions of several of the voices recorded by Mayhew and re-arranged them as a kind of narrative poem-sequence.

LUTZ SEILER was born in Thuringia in 1963 and now lives in Wilhelmshorst near Berlin, where he manages the Peter Huchel House, former home of the poet Peter Huchel, which now serves as monument to his memory and as literary centre. Lutz Seiler has published two collections, *pech & blende* (2000) and *vierzig kilometer nacht* (2003), and a collection of essays *Sonntags dachte ich an Gott* (2004) — all published by Suhrkamp Verlag, Frankfurt.

SPENCER SELBY lives in Oakland, California. He was born and raised in the midwest of the USA, started SINK Press in the early 1980s and co-ordinated the Cannessa Park Reading Series from 1987-1993. He is the author of seven volumes of poetry, three of visual poetry, and a study of film noir called *Dark City* (McFarland & Co, 1997, 2nd edition).

ANJA UTLER lives in Vienna, but comes from Germany. She won the Leonce-und-Lena Prize for poets under the age of 35 in 2003 — the major award of its kind for young poets in the German-speaking world. The 'Sibyl' poem is drawn from her first full-length collection *münden — entzüngeln* (Edition Korrespondenzen, Franz Hammerbacher, Vienna, 2004). The German text is also available online at www.lyrikline.de, together with a recording of the author reading the poem.

Better known for his prose than his verse, the Swiss writer ROBERT WALSER (1878-1956) was first and foremost a poet. Poems of his were appearing in newspapers for a decade before his collection *Gedichte* (Poems) was published in 1909 by Bruno Cassirer in Berlin. That bibliophile edition (only 300 copies), with vignettes etched by Karl Walser, was even re-issued, though in a smaller format, in 1919. Four verse playlets, *Komödie* (Comedy) followed in 1920. The ample body of his subsequent verse now fills volume XI of the *Das Gesamtwerk* (The Collected Works). Among the 'microscripts' of 1921-33 there are also dozens of poems, now in volumes 4 and 6 of *Aus dem Bleistiftgebiet* (From the Pencil Zone, Suhrkamp Verlag, Frankfurt, 1985-2000): some from the latter source were translated in *PN Review* 140 in 2001. Three of the poems here were not chosen for their oddity alone — Walser wrote plenty of prose but very few poems relating to other writers, or about artists. He probably met with Jules Rascin late during his Berlin period (1905-1913). Rilke had been buried only two days before the poem to him was published. [*Note by Christopher Middleton.*]

MARK WEISS is the author of six books of poetry, most recently *Fieldnotes* (Junction Press, 1995) and *Figures: 32 Poems* (Chax Press, Tucson, 2001), and *Different Birds* (Shearsman Books ebook, 2004). He runs Junction Press in San Diego and is particularly active as a translator from Spanish. In 2003 he co-edited with Harry Polkinhorn the volume *Across the Line / Al otro lado*, a bilingual anthology of poetry from Baja California. He is currently editing an anthology of modern Cuban poetry. His translations of Jose Kozer will appear in the next issue of the magazine.

RECENT & FORTHCOMING PUBLICATIONS BY SHEARSMAN BOOKS

All Isbns for the books listed here begin with 0-907562-. Just add the first three numbers inside the brackets to get the correct individual ISBN.

Anthony Barnett	*Miscanthus: Selected and New Poems*	(55-8, £11.95/$17.95)
Kelvin Corcoran	*New and Selected Poems*	(39-6, £10.95/$16.95)
M.T.C. Cronin	*<More or Less Than> 1-100*	(47-7, £9.95/$15.95)
Ian Davidson	*At a Stretch*	(44-2, £8.95 /$13.95)
Peter Dent	*Handmade Equations*	(65-5, £8.95/$13.95)
Laurie Duggan	*Compared to What. Selected Poems 1971-2003*	(61-2, £11.95/$20)
Laurie Duggan	*The Ash Range*	(61-2, £12.95/$21)
Gloria Gervitz	*Migrations* (translated by Mark Schafer)	(49-3, £15.95)
Lee Harwood	*Collected Poem*	(40-X, £17.95/$28)
Ralph Hawkins	*The MOON, The Chief Hairdresser (highlights)*	
		(42-6, £8.95/$13.95)
David Jaffin	*These Time-Shifting Thoughts*	(68-X, £7.50/$12)
Trevor Joyce	*with the first dream of fire they hunt the cold* (2nd edition)	(37-X, £11.95/$18)
Rupert M. Loydell	*A Conference of Voices*	(56-6, £9.95/$15.95)
Christopher Middleton	*Palavers, & A Nocturnal Journal*	(51-5, £9.95/ $15.95)
David Miller	*The Waters of Marah*	(66-3, £8.95)
John Muckle	*Firewriting and other poems*	(64-7, £9.95/$15.95)
Peter Philpott	*Textual Possessions*	(53-1, £9.95/$15.95)
Tessa Ransford (ed./trrans.)	*The Nightingale Question*	(52-3, £8.95/$13.95)
Peter Riley	*The Dance at Mociu* (prose)	(36-1, £8.95/$13.95)
Lisa Samuels	*Paradise for Everyone*	(67-1, £8.95/$14)
John Seed	*Pictures from Mayhew. London 1850*	(62-0, £10.95/$18)
John Seed	*New and Collected Poems*	(63-9, £9.95/$16)
Michael Smith	*Maldon & Other Translations*	(60-4, £9.95/$15.95)
Michael Smith	*The Purpose of the Gift. Selected Poems*	(59-0, £9.95/$15.95)
Harriet Tarlo	*Poems 1990-2003*	(45-0, £9.95/$15.95)
Dirk van Bastelaere	*The Last to Leave – Selected Poems* (trans. by W. Groenewegen, J. Irons and F. R. Jones)	(70-1, £9.95/$16)
John Welch	*The Eastern Boroughs*	(53-4, £9.95/$15.95)
David Wevill	*Departures. Selected Poems*	(34-5, £9.95/$15)

Coming Soon:

Tom Lowenstein	*Ancestors and Species. Selected Ethnographic Poetry*	(Oct. 2005, 74-4, £9.95/$16)
Ilma Rakusa	*A Farewell to Everything* (trans. by Andrew Shields & Andrew Winnard)	(Oct. 2005, 53-4, £9.95/$16)
Elaine Randell	*New and Selected Poems*	(Nov. 2005, 71-X, £9.95/$16)

César Vallejo	_Trilce_, (translated by Michael Smith & Valentino Gianuzzi)	(Sep 2005, 72-8, £12.95/$21)
César Vallejo	_The Complete Later Poems, 1923-1938_, (transl. by Gianuzzi & Smith)	(Sep. 2005, 73-6, £16.95/$28)
Catherine Walsh	_As Lathair. Selected Books_	(June 2005, 58-2, £10.95/$18)
Catherine Walsh	_City West & Optic Verve_	(June 2005, 54-X, £9.95/$16)
Nigel Wheale	_New and Selected Poems_	(Nov. 2005, 75-2, £9.95/$16)

Books to look out for in 2006 include volumes by Martin Anderson, Ian Davidson, Peter Finch, Christopher Gutkind, Sarah Law, Janet Sutherland, and Scott Thurston, in addition to several more volumes in translation. The next double-issue of _Shearsman_ magazine will appear in October 2005.

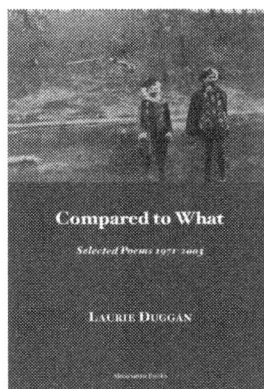

May 2005
223pp, Paperback
9x6ins, £11.95 / $20
ISBN 0-907562-61-2

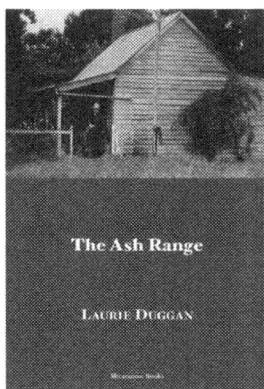

May 2005
247pp, Paperback
9x6ins, £12.95 / $21
ISBN 0-907562-69-8

April 2005
171pp, Paperback
8.5x5.5ins, £10.95 / $18
ISBN 0-907562-62-0

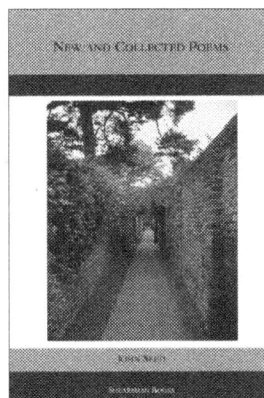

(left) April 2005
155pp, Paperback
8.5x5.5ins, £9.95 / $16
ISBN 0-907562-63-9

(right) April 2005
118pp, Paperback,
8.5x5.5ins, £9.95 / $16
ISBN 0-907562-70-1

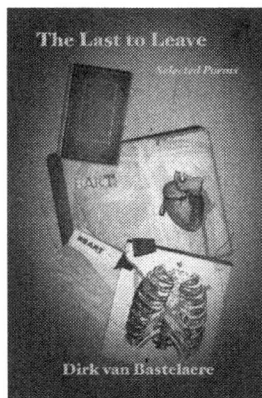

www.ingramcontent.com/pod-product-compliance
Lightning Source LLC
Chambersburg PA
CBHW031004090426
42737CB00008B/672